Golden Age
and Viking Art
in Sweden

Golden Age in Sweden

Contents

and Viking Art

Preface

The sea raids of the Scandinavian Vikings have been brought into prominence this year by the publication of the medieval map of the world in the possession of the Yale University. In this map America not only bears the name "Vinland" but also is said to have been discovered by the Vikings "Björn and Leif together". The Vikings have won fame mainly as sea farers, warriors and pirates. Using the mighty Russian waterways they made their way to the Mediterranean, and they raided Normandy and England. From Norway they colonized Iceland and Greenland, whence – long before Columbus – they reached the American continent.

The exhibition whose material is now shown for the first time outside Scandinavia presents another and less known aspect of the Vikings, namely their artistic capacity. But the works of art exhibited are not confined to the Viking Era (c. 800–1050 A.D.). They also cover parts of the epoch which is usually named the Migration Period (c. 100–800 A.D.). Some scholars have called this period the Scandinavian Golden Age. Swedish finds from that time contain astonishingly large quantities of gold. What is remarkable is that the principal part of this gold was worked in Sweden and that the jewels and mounts which have been preserved show an artistic quality and a technical skill which also help to justify the name, the Golden Age.

Where did all this gold come from? No gold deposits of importance were discovered in Sweden until the 1920s. Some of the wealth, of course, may emanate from the raids of the Vikings and their forefathers. But we know, too, that these men were also capable and successful merchants. This is stated in the laconic words on the rune-stones raised to men who acquired riches in Greece and Gårdarike (Russia), who traded in furs with the southern lands and "fared far after gold".

During their long voyages the men from the North came into contact with, among others, the highly cultured peoples of the Mediterranean regions. It is, however, striking how little they were influenced by antique art. Certain jewels (e.g. Plate XV) imitate Roman coins in a primitive way. The Northmen seem to have received a somewhat deeper impression from the ornamental art of the East, although this does not mean that one can speak of any direct stylistic influence from that quarter.

What is so remarkable is that in their gold- and silver-smith's work the Northmen developed a style of ornament – sometimes highly distinctive – that was peculiarly their own and that this style was of a high decorative standard. As Professor Holmqvist points out in his introduction, animal ornaments dominate the whole of the period covered by the exhibition. Exotic animals, dragons, lions and birds are stylized and intertwined to form a strange, abstract and almost surrealistic type of composition. Sometimes there are images of human beings, primitively stylized, but strangely enough we almost never find plant ornaments. How these animal ornaments arose and developed is a question which has not yet been fully answered. They also occurs in different forms in continental Europe, Ireland and the British Isles, but nowhere are they so imaginative and so varied as in the Nordic territories. Some scholars maintain that Nordic art gave the origin to the animal style. From a purely technical point of view the consummate ability of the Nordic artists cannot fail to impress the beholder. In many of the objects the precision in the details is so great that you will need a microscope to be able to appreciate the fine ornaments. For this reason the exhibition has been supplemented with greatly enlarged photographs of details which reveal the richness of the ornaments and the technical accuracy of the craftsmen – all the more amazing as it was achieved at a time when there were no magnifying glasses.

When this exhibition, Golden Age and Viking Art in Sweden, was first shown in the Museum of National Antiquities, Stockholm, it aroused great interest among both specialists and the general public. Now that it has

5

ventured forth over the Atlantic, we hope that with its representative selection it will meet with a similarly favourable reception. Modern Scandinavian applied art has already won appreciation in the United States of America. This exhibition shows that we have ancient traditions to look back upon and that they can serve as a constant source of inspiration.

Gösta Selling

Introduction

In that grey hour before the dawn of history in Northern Europe – grey because of its remoteness and our incomplete knowledge of it – there is nevertheless a gleam of light in the darkness, a golden side of which we quite often get strange and fascinating glimpses. These glimpses are vouchsafed to us on the occasions when prehistoric gold and silver hoards are found in the Nordic lands and we suddenly find ourselves in the presence of artistic creations executed with admirable skill, ornamental and figural compositions which throw new light on the epoch in which they were made, and give us new insights into the conditions of life at that time, into the cultural standard and the relations with foreign lands.

All too frequently these ancient treasures are presented merely as cultural objects intended to throw light on a whole era together with quantities of other objects. It is worth observing in passing that they have a value of their own, that they have much to tell us of the eternal struggle of the artist with his materials and of his efforts to give a living interpretation of his own times.

In the following pages a short account will be given of the techniques employed in art metalwork in prehistoric times. Even if space permitted it would not be possible to give a full description, for the simple reason that research has not yet been able to discover all the techniques used by prehistoric craftsmen; indeed, we are still far from knowing all the tools they used for their work.

In these pages and also, of course, in the exhibition of original objects which they are intended to illuminate, the reader can study a Nordic art in being and a Nordic art which at the same time is at a peak of achievement which it is difficult altogether to understand and, of course, still more difficult to explain.

Nordic art reflects many different influences when it emerges into our notice during the first centuries A.D. It

7

shows a marked dependence on the Roman art world as this was manifested in the Mediterranean region and in the provinces of the Empire. It also shows the sympathy of a related mentality for Celtic taste and stylistic feeling, prominent in the crafts as practised in Gaul and in the British Isles. But it also shows another element of a fundamental and decisive nature, namely, an influence from the art of Eastern Europe, where the Greek inheritance still survived, where the art and culture of the Asian steppe peoples could be studied at close quarters and where Sarmatians and Goths were the connecting links with the rest of Europe, as also with the Nordic regions.

It is easy to look upon the first centuries of the Christian era as a training period during which the Nordic craftsman gained practice in all the multifarious techniques in which he was later to show such mastery. He learned how to chase and engrave, to do niello and embossed work, repoussé, etc., as well as the arts of filigree, granulation and cloisonné. If the results sometimes seem modest to our eyes, we should not forget that by comparison with his counterpart in more southerly lands the Nordic artist had a small and scattered clientele and could not look to big governmental commissions for his support.

It is therefore all the more surprising that during the great era of the 5th and 6th centuries the Nordic artist was able to show so much independence in the presence of so many possible models. It is now that Germanic animal ornament emerges. From the point of view of art history this is undoubtedly a great and remarkable event. Something like fifteen hundred years before the surrealism and disolution of natural forms familiar to us in modern art, there was being created in Northern Europe a new conception of form which shows a radical break with the old and which at the same time lent itself admirably to all the artist's intentions. To venture this leap from the naturalism of antique tradition to a symbolistic unreality of figurative details disposed about the decorative surface in the same way we find among many of our modern artists must for these first Germanic masters have been a greater feat, if this be possible, than the Palaeolithic cave paintings were during still more remote times. Even if the humanism imbued in us by our classical education may prevent us from understanding the true essence of Germanic animal ornament, we must nevertheless be impressed by the skill of the anonymous artists, by the superb formulation of the individual details, by the excitement and vitality, by the lively imagination shown in their works.

The immense power of survival of this animal ornament can be realized when we note that it dominated Nordic art from the 5th century to the 12th, a period of 700 years, and that among the peasantry it lived on far into the Middle Ages.

Over such a long period it is natural that animal ornament should show many different variations and present many different types of content and feeling. It can be soft and elegiac, calm and majestic, nervous and full of tension, baroque and overpowering, demonic and full of aggressions, lyrically romantic and academically ceremonious. A close study of its products often reveals unsuspected qualities and gives us a deeper insight into the period during which they were created, as well as into the intentions and temperament of the artists who made them.

It was the Nordic artist who was the principal contributor to this type of ornament and also its most diligent practitioner. It is a remarkable as well as an important fact that for a long period it was to constitute a dominant feature in the artistic practice of the rest of Europe as well, from the British Isles in the west to Italy and Austria in the south. It mingles with other styles and has an offshoot in the miniatures of the manuscripts, it survives in new forms and fertilizes artistic creation for centuries.

"An Age of Gold". If the period deserves that name, was it an era of prosperity? Yes, undoubtedly. Without a measure of prosperity it is difficult for art to live. When the struggle for existence is too pressing art is pushed aside, to return when the struggle has succeeded. Exactly how "golden" that era of prehistory was with which we are here concerned is something that we can actually weigh and measure. Never has gold come in such steady streams to the Nordic countries as during the epoch which can justly be called an age of gold, the 5th and 6th centuries A.D. Since the Nordic countries themselves did not produce gold, they must necessarily have been in a position to give something else in exchange in order to indulge in the luxury of buying or otherwise acquiring this costly metal.

Probably the gold came, mostly in the form of coins minted in the eastern or western halves of the Roman Empire, so-called solidi. We find evidence of the general prosperity, for example, in the latest available survey about gold coin finds on the islands of Gotland, Öland and Bornholm, with 245, 272 and 152 coins respectively, or of individual coin hoards such as, for example, 80 coins from Åby, Sandby parish, Öland, 79 from Botes, Ethelhem parish, Gotland, or 47 from Helgö, Uppland. The impression becomes still greater, however, when we convert the unminted gold into solidi. The massive gold neck ring from Trolleberg in Skåne has a weight equal to about 284 solidi, our largest preserved gold hoard, that from Timboholm in Västergötland, corresponds to no fewer than 1,614 solidi and the treasure from Tureholm, V. Ljung, Södermanland, to nearly 3,000 solidi. These must be regarded as representing quite considerable values. Perhaps, however, the figures become a little less impressive when we remember that in A.D. 443 Theodosius II paid Attila 432,000 solidi in order to be left in peace, or that when the Byzantian emperor Anastasius died in A.D. 518 he left a gold treasure weighing about 128,000; but on the other hand the Roman army was able to buy back captured legionaries at the relatively modest price of 8 solidi each.

Nevertheless we must regard the flow of solidi to the Nordic territories, the many and large gold hoards, the heavy and magnificent gold jewels, as evidence of prosperity and of a golden age, at least for those in authority and along with them – perhaps – for artists and craftsmen as well.

A similar prosperity marks the Viking era. Then, too, it is easy to measure prosperity in coins and it may be of interest to mention some statistics of the Swedish finds. In Sweden no fewer than about 100,000 Arabian silver coins – whole specimens or parts – minted in the 8th, 9th and 10th centuries have been discovered. We have found about 57,000 German silver coins and about 33,000 English ones, mainly from the 10th and 11th centuries. In addition there are fragments of coins, Byzantian coins, etc., which like the earlier solidi show that the flow persisted. Of individual silver hoards, one of the largest, that from Buttle parish, Gotland, contains no fewer than 2,673 Arabian silver coins, a treasure from Johannishus, Hjortsberga, Blekinge, contains more than 4,000 coins, mainly German and English, and a treasure from Äspinge in Hurva parish, Skåne, has 8,700 silver coins. If we compare with these the hoards of unminted silver the difference is not so great as that between minted and unminted gold hoards from an earlier epoch. The reason for this is no doubt that it had become increasingly usual to use minted precious metals as a means of payment.

The figures given here of Swedish silver hoards may perhaps seem impressive enough, but they pale into relative insignificance before the fact that in A.D. 991 the English had to pay the invading Norsemen the sum of 10,000 pounds of silver, in 994 16,000 pounds, in 1002 24,000 pounds, in 1007 36,000 pounds and in 1012 no less than 48,000 pounds. Taking a pound to be equal to about 4 hectogrammes the last payment would thus amount to about 20,000 kilogrammes of silver. One or two other statistics may be given here. In the 9th century the governor of Chorasan delivered to the Caliph every year 40–50 million dirhems, thas is to say 120–150 tons of silver, and it is calculated that the total income of the Caliph around the year 800 was no less than 400 million dirhems, or 1,200 tons of silver. The reader no doubt asks: Where has all this silver gone to?

And yet it is the Nordic countries that seem, relatively speaking, to have preserved most of this abundant flow until the present day. In the more than 700 Swedish silver hoards there are, for example, more German and English silver coins than are preserved in the minting countries themselves, and probably the same is true of Arabian coins.

We can therefore justifiably speak of a golden and, for that matter, a silver prehistoric era in Northern Europe, an era of prosperity which provided a fertile ground for artistic creation in many different types of materials. The rich inheritance which this age has handed on to posterity is doubly valuable to scholars since it belongs to an epoch for which there are no written records. In the intricate figures of animal ornament among symbols and human figures, carved, hammered and soldered in precious metals, we can, however, not only discern the skill of the master hand but we can also spell out some lines of the ancient story, which was the golden age of the Nordic peoples before the dawn of history in these regions.

WILHELM HOLMQVIST

Casting

Casting, one of the oldest metallurgical techniques, was practised in the Nordic region from the beginning of the Bronze Age onwards. For simpler objects the craftsmen used open or two-part moulds, often made of soapstone or sandstone. More complicated objects were cast by the technique known as cire perdue (lost wax). First, a wax model of the desired object was made and this model was surrounded by clay, forming a mould. Fine-grained sand or crushed pottery was added to the clay in order to give it a porous structure, this being necessary to prevent the mould from shrinking when the clay dried and from cracking in the subsequent heating When heat was applied the wax melted and ran away in specially made channels. The mould was now ready for casting. The molten metal was poured down and occupied the space left by the wax model. After this the mould was cooled and broken up and the cast object could be removed and worked on. In this processing the object acquired its final form: the casting seams were polished away and decoration could be applied with a punch or graver.

Cire-perdue casting was used during the whole of the Iron Age. There are, however, certain indications that during the later Iron Age two-part mould of clay began to be used to an increasing extent. This is probably connected with the adaption of a new fashion in jewellery, involving the wearing of brooches in pairs. It was obviously desirable that these brooches should be identical, but this was difficult to achieve with the cire-perdue technique. The rich decoration aimed at also made it impossible to use stone moulds, since it would be difficult to carve the finer details of the ornament in such a material. The craftsmen therefore began to make two-part moulds of clay which, as in the case of cire perdue casting, was made porous by adding sand or pottery fragments. On many of the brooches which were worn in pairs we can see on the reverse side clear impressions of cloth. These impressions have, probably quite correctly, been connected with the technique of casting in two-part claymoulds. The theory is that the casting was done by first making a solid model of the object, usually in wax but sometimes perhaps in clay. The model was submerged into the soft clay which was to form the upper half of the mould. The clay was then allowed to dry with the wax model in position. Afterwards the mould was heated slightly, causing the wax to become fluid. With the aid of a piece of cloth the craftsman now removed surplus wax so that only as much of the wax was left as corresponded to the desired thickness of the cast object. Next the clay which was to form the lower half of the mould was applied. This section was provided with wedges which fitted into specially made depressions in the upper section. The piece of cloth which had been used to remove the surplus wax remained behind. After the lower section had received the impression of the thinned wax model it could be lifted off with the aid of the cloth and dried. In the process of drying the cloth probably served to prevent the impression of the mould shrinking to any great extent. The mould sections were then burnt slightly, after that both the wax and the cloth was removed, and the mould wax ready for casting. However, the lower section now carried the impression of the cloth which can still be seen on the back of the brooches. The mould was bound together with metal wire, the holes were filled with clay and the molten metal was poured in the ingot. The mould was embedded in sand in order to reduce the risk of its cracking when heated. After cooling, the mould was opened. At this stage the lower half of the mould was probably broken but the upper section could be kept more or less intact so that it could be used again after minor repairs. Because the pattern in the soft clay could easily be worn away the produce could not, however, be repeated more than once or twice. One can also often observe that one of the brooches in a set has a less distinct pattern than the other, probably because the mould had suffered from wear. The suggestion has also been made that even the two-part moulds were used only once and that the close similarities between the products were due to the fact that these were clay patterns which could be used several times. It is not improbable that this was sometimes done, but the procedure would have been so time-consuming and complicated that the simpler wax procedure would no doubt have been preferred in most cases. A number of more or less intact upper moulds have been found, whereas fragments which can be shown to have belonged to lower sections, that is to say, on which cloth impressions remain, are rare.

The fragments of cast moulds which have been preserved show that even extremely fine details could be produced already at the casting stage. The surprising thing here is that among other things the craftsmen seem to have produced stamp ornamentation in casting, as is shown by, for example, a mould for a serpent brooch from Helgö. On this fragment we can see thin ring stamps which were clearly cast and not stamped on afterwards. Probably a very large proportion of the stamped decoration on bronze objects from the later Germanic Iron Age was produced in this way.

Patterns for the cast objects were probably made from wood as well as from wax and possibly clay. This might be one of the explanations why in the animal ornament on metallic objects we often find features which seem to have been taken more or less directly from the art of wood carving. The close correspondence between the wood carvings on the Viking-era boat grave from Oseberg in Norway and contemporary metalwork also shows us that these two kinds of art are connected with each other. It is very probable that such wood models were used for producing the more complicated interlace which we find on, for example, the edges of some 7th–8th century-brooches. But at the same time we can establish in other objects that a very large part of the decoration has been done after casting. Probably no fixed rules were followed, each master having his own way of working. Thus in the case of some objects all or nearly all the decoration was produced in the mould whereas in others the decoration was applied after the object had been cast.   BIRGIT ARRHENIUS

Engraving

Engraving is perhaps at once the simplest and the most common of all the techniques used in prehistoric art metalwork. Its main purpose is to produce decoration on a metal surface by incisions, possibly just as a pattern of lines or in some cases as a deeper relief with a more plastic effect. A distinction is therefore made between line engraving and relief engraving. The artist uses gravers or burins, i.e. sharp-edged tools of different shapes according to the particular purpose for which they are needed. Among other tools used by present-day engravers are chisels, pitch blocks, cushions, magnifying glasses, etc., and it may be presumed that their prehistoric forerunners used tools of broadly similar kinds.

Engraving as a technique has much in common with wood carving and consequently one often finds in metal objects effects which originated with another material. Among these are line carving, flat cutting, chip carving, etc. Artistically, of course, the craftsman aims to produce in the metal surface a maximum of light-refraction effects to cause the costly metal to catch the eye with a multitude of lines and surfaces which are kept together only by the predetermined pattern. *Figs. IV, V, VI, VII a, IX*

This surface decoration finds its most distinctive form in chip carving, a form of relief engraving with deep V-shaped incisions. Here as a rule the artist follows a geometric basic pattern composed with the aid of rule and compass. The pattern may consist of vortex motifs, star and rosette motifs, triangles, squares, pyramids, zig-zag and meander borders with sharply chipcarved surfaces meeting one another at acute angles. The resultant interchange of different lights and shades constitutes, as it were a victory over the very weight of the metal, and this indeed is the artist's aim. *Fig. IX*

It was not only geometric motifs that could be presented in this way. Tendrils in relief engraving were also common, and above all in the Nordic lands we find animal ornament in chip carving of the most beautiful kind.

Mould forms and semi-manufactured products found in the Nordic territories indicate that in relief engraving the artist often started with an object whose basic shape had been produced by casting. All the details were added by hand engraving. Obviously the details could also be cast, at least in their main outlines, but in any case what was produced by casting called for careful processing involving the use of both the graver and a polishing tool. In the surface decoration of Nordic prehistoric metalwork objects we find represented all the intermediate forms between purely cast and purely engraved work.

Tremolier engraving is a method by which the artist drove the graver forward while twisting the cutting edge from side to side. In this way he produced a zig-zag line, the "pitch" of the zig-zag depending on the angle at which the graver was applied to the surface.

Historical Development

The engraving of metal objects is a technique as old as the metal objects themselves and we find it among all peoples and in all countries. It therefore seems unnecessary to mention here any particular examples from different cultures except in so far as these throw light on Nordic conditions.

The earliest evidences of metal engraving in Northern Europe do not occur until the later phase of the Bronze Age, 600–500 B.C. It then emerges in the unassuming form of tremolier work and is quite certainly inspired by the engraving art which had developed very much earlier in the more southerly parts of Europe.

Engraving did not have its breakthrough in Northern Europe until the late Roman era, i.e. in the 4th century A.D. During the following centuries it flourished greatly, though the reason for this is not fully clear; probably it is to be seen against the background of certain developments in European art as a whole. At this period European art was naturally dominated by Roman taste and style, and far beyond the boundaries of the Empire Roman products were imitated in different ways and in different materials. Roman art itself was going through a phase where stylized and geometric designs were fashionable. Its practitioners were turning increasingly away from the idealizing forms which had been inherited from classical Greek art and were creating an art based on rule and compass, a geometric style which spread widely, not only within the boundaries of the Empire but also, and perhaps especially, among the Germanic peoples. In the Roman territories the geometric style appears in architectural decoration, in mosaics and textiles, and in metalwork.

The technique of engraving was well adapted to such a style and so for this reason also we find innumerable late Roman art products with engraved star motifs and circle rosettes, vortex motifs and square patterns, geometric tendrils, and so on. Often this engraving occurs together with other techniques such as niello work, stamped decoration, gilding, and so on. (See following section.)

At least three different types of products can be distinguished in this late Roman metalwork.

1. Silver objects which have been given their basic form by casting and have subsequently been decorated with rich engraving in the geometric style. The engraving is shallow and considerable parts of it are inlaid with niello. It is also partially gilded, either by means of applied gold leaf or by fire gilding. Stamped decoration is also found.

2. Silver objects which have similarly been cast in their basic shape and subsequently furnished with rich engraving in a geometric style, this, however, being supplemented later with tendril and animal ornament. The engraving is *deep* – chip carving – and only to a minor extent inlaid with niello. It is likewise partially gilded by means of fire gilding. Stamped decoration also occurs.

3. Bronze objects which have been cast complete with all their essential details in chip-carving and geometric style supplemented by tendril and animal ornament. A central medallion field has engraved decoration in the form of animal figures, human busts, etc. – This group

of objects are collectively described as late Roman chip-carved bronzes.

All the categories here mentioned have counterparts in Germanic and, above all, Nordic areas. The first category Fig. X has its counterpart in the Nordic "Sösdala" style during the 5th century A.D. and the second category, which is undoubtedly the most important, has a counterpart in what has been called the "Sjörup" style and comprises a quantity of the best Nordic goldsmiths' work from the 5th and 6th centuries A.D.

The theory has been put forward that these last-mentioned objects, that is to say the big Nordic relief brooches of silver gild, sword scabbard mounts in the same material, etc., were cast only in their basic shape and then later engraved individually. In support of this theory is adduced the fact that hardly any two of these objects have exactly the same decoration, as, of course, would have been the case if they had been cast in the same mould. Furthermore, in Norway there has been found a mould form which has only the rough shape of a relief brooch without any indication of decoration.

There is undoubtedly much to indicate that the engraver played an important part in the work of producing objects made of precious metals, but it does not seem to be possible to accept the idea that these were created entirely with the aid of the engraving tool. On the Continent there have been found bronze casting patterns that are finished in details, and in the Nordic countries there have been encountered mould forms of burnt clay on which even quite minor ornamental details are present. So far as is known no wooden or wax patterns have been found, although it must be assumed that such models were used.

During the period which follows the great era of the Fig. IV–VI, IX relief brooch, i.e. from the 7th century A.D. onwards, engraving is still abundantly used in Nordic art, partly for the trimming of cast chip-carving decoration, for carving frames and mouldings, for shallow engraving of surface ornament, for tremolier work, for excision in connection with niello and other inlaid work.

WILHELM HOLMQVIST

Chasing

Whereas engraving is a form of decoration which may be said to consist in cutting away certain parts of a metallic surface in order that a desired pattern may appear, chasing involves the modelling or partial hammering of the metal so that the pattern envisaged may appear in relief. The tools used in this technique are various kinds of hammers, mallets and punches. In addition use is made of a ball of pitch resting in a leather ring. The pitch may also, of course, be spread on a flat base. Iron hammers are used in connection with a soft base, hammers of wood or horn with a harder base. Both punches and hammers may be of many different kinds, the former usually being made individually according to the needs of the product. A present-day craftsman may have hundreds of punches and seldom has fewer than 50–70.

As a rule the work is done both from the front and the back of the object and involves repeated heating (annealing) of the metal, which in the process of hammering and punching tends to become hard and brittle.

The technical aids and the working procedures seem to have been largely the same during prehistoric times as in our own days, as is shown by the extant material. Unfortunately, however, the tools used in the work have been preserved to a far smaller extent than the finished products.

Historical Development

The art of producing chased gold and silver objects is very ancient. The famous royal graves at Ur from the third millennium B.C. contain exquisite specimens, in the form of helmets, drinking vessels, etc. The Egyptian Pharaohs also surrounded themselves with costly and luxurious articles of this kind, which in their most impressive form are represented by, for example, the rich treasures from the tomb of Tutankhamen from the 14th century B.C. In the Cretan, Greek and Roman cultures we find splendid examples of this art. Far out on the periphery of classical culture, among the nomadic Scythians, craftsmen worked on gold with hammers and punches, transforming it into objects of impressive and, at the same time, highly individual character.

In the Nordic territories the decoration of gold objects by chasing had a modest beginning. We can, however, refer to, among other things, the chased gold foils which decorate brooches and swords from the well-known Håga mound in Uppland, Sweden, as well as other similar objects from the period around 1000 B.C. There are, moreover, from the same period or immediately after it collars and tweezers of bronze with chased boss ornament. Small chased bronze vessels from the same period also occur.

From the period around the beginning of the Christian era come a large number of cauldrons, some of which are made of bronze only but most of which are of bronze and iron. It is not known whether these were imported but there is much to indicate that at any rate the composite cauldrons were of Nordic manufacture. These cauldrons bear eloquent witness to the difficulties the craftsmen had to deal with. It was relatively easy to hammer out a bowl or bronze plate, although the hammer blows are both clearly visible and uneven. But in order to arrive at the final shape the craftsman had to use an iron band which formed the upper part of the vessel and was fastened to the bronze bowl with a large number of rivets.

Of the other bronze vessels from this period and the first centuries of the Christian era which have been found in Nordic countries it is likely that all, or at any rate most, were imported from Roman art industry centres.

A number of silver beakers, most of them found in Denmark, belonging to the 2nd and 3rd centuries A.D., are generally regarded as Nordic chased work. So far as can be judged they were cast in their basic form and then cold-hammered. A Swedish beaker of this kind has chased fluting. From the same period we also find small, thimble-like
Fig. VII b chased calottes for decorative rivets on shield bosses and

shield handles which are particularly common in the art industry of Öland.

After this it is not until well into the Viking era that we again find chased vessels in Nordic metalwork. In Denmark there have been found a number of silver bowls and beakers which can be stated with certainty to be Nordic works from the Viking era, and in Sweden there are several hoard finds from the period of transition to the Middle Ages with chased silver bowls of Nordic manufacture.

In more purely ornamental art there is wider scope for chased objects. Here it is mainly a question of metal foils which are placed as decorative elements on jewels and other objects. As a rule, however, the decoration on these metal foils seems to have been produced by pressing the foil against a pattern with the intended decoration. Several such patterns of bronze have been found in the Nordic countries.

Such pressed foils are already common in the period around the beginning of the Christian era and from the following few centuries we also find them in both bronze and silver. They may have a simple geometric decoration but not infrequently they also have isolated animal figures or rows of such figures.

During the 5th and 6th centuries the pressed-foil technique was used increasingly in the service of the ever more dominant animal ornament and the 7th and 8th centuries bring a real flowering of this art with an extraordinarily richly developed ornament in this technique. From the same period come some dies with figural motifs, the well-known bronze plates from Torslunda on Öland. These patterns were intended for, among other things, the figural pressed foils which decorated the temple band on the contemporary Nordic helmets.

The small figural gold foils wich were found on Helgö in Sweden and at Hauge, Klepp, in Norway, as well as other places, are somewhat problematic, inasmuch as of 26 specimens found on Helgö only two seem to be from the same pattern, and the same seems to be true of the Norwegian gold foils. One cannot avoid thinking that they

Fig. vii a

Fig. xxi a

Fig. xii

Fig. xxi a

Fig. xii

bine motifs from two different dies. In the course of the development the central images on the bracteates become very varied and give us a brilliant insight into a peculiarly Nordic pictorial art, limited by reason of its technique but nevertheless expressive. The pictorial content often has a riddle-like form which probably could only be understood by the initiated. Around the central image there may often run stamped borders which present a rich variety of motifs. Only with the aid of a magnifying glass is it possible to discover the ridges between the stamps in the concentric borders; the precision with which these are executed almost gives the impression that the decoration has been unitarily designed for the whole surface. In contrast with the central image, the borders have been struck from the front. They are often richly composed.

Fig. IV A considerably coarser stamped decoration, but one equally rich in variations, is found on mounts and brooches of gilded bronze from the 6th and 7th centuries. Here there are several features which indicate that the decoration was not stamped on the metal with a punch but was cast, i.e. the stamped motif had already been applied to the mould form.

Fig. XIII In other cases the craftsman probably carved out a depression in the metal surface to receive the stamp. Such a procedure would, among other things, explain the decoration on a couple of large gold rings from the early Germanic Iron Age where the stamps are imprinted in very deep depressions.

In the rich repertoire of different types of stamped motifs that a Nordic goldsmith commanded during the Iron Age – of which many were specifically Nordic – a stamp in the form of a Y-shaped figure is, for all its simplicity, one of the most elegant which has been found in the field of stamped decoration.

This type of stamp was employed during the latter half of the 8th century. Other stamps also show different frequencies of use during different phases and it appears as if stamped ornament was as fixed in its style as was Nordic animal ornament.

BIRGIT ARRHENIUS

Incrustation

The word "incrustation" is derived from the Italian *crosta,* hard surface or crust. The term describes a procedure which involves the decoration of a metallic surface by hammering on or inlaying a metal of another colour. If the metal is simply hammered on to a slightly roughened metallic surface the procedure is often called "false incrustation", whereas true incrustation is characterized by the decorative metal being actually inlaid in the base surface.

Incrustation occurs in a number of different variations. One method is to cut out the desired motif in the metal surface with a graver in such a way that the cut edges are Fig. xxi a not vertical but are inclined inwards at an angle towards each other. In this way the metal that is hammered in to the groove is kept in place by the overhanging edges of the host metal.

Another way is to cut a deep spiral groove in the metal round for instance a cylinder-shaped object while continually inserting and hammering in the decorative metal wire. If desired the spiral can be made so tight and the metal wire so thick that the decorative metal can be hammered out so as to produce the effect of covering the whole surface, that is to say the same effect as in *plating.* The spiral can, however, be less dense and in this case Fig. xxi b the procedure is repeated, but in the reverse direction; new grooves in the metal surface are cut out *over* the already inserted metal wires while continually hammering in more wires, possibly of a third metal. After the subsequent polishing there appears a simple pattern of differently coloured metals.

In the *surface-filling* metal overlay produced by incrustation, decorations of different types can be incised. First the intended pattern is lightly engraved and then the lines are deepened and in some cases filled with niello. If it is desired to introduce yet another metal, for example gold, the metal surface is roughened at the places where it is intended to put the gold, after which this is hammered on.

In the case of certain incrusted works, both of the finer and the simpler variety, use has been made of metal foils stamped on with a die, the other parts of the metal surface being left intact. It was also possible, of course, to roughen the parts of the metal surface which it was desired to decorate, to hammer on the metal foil and then burnish the surface.

Historical Development

Ever since mankind acquired a knowledge of more than one metal artists have tried to combine the different metals with one another. In the territories between the two great rivers, the Euphrates and the Tigris, the art of incrustation was already known during the third millennium B.C., although it did not become very generally used. Thus in one of the Sumerian royal graves at Ur there has been found a silver bowl the surface of which shows a network of broad electrum wires polished in. (Electrum is an alloy of gold and silver.) In Egypt there have been finds of numerous bronze objects incrusted with gold or silver and dating from the 12th and 13th dynasties, i.e. from the first half of the second millennium B.C. But it is later, in the Greek cultural world, that we find the most exquisite specimens of prehistoric incrustation. We may mention the splendid weapons of the Mycenaean graves with their animal figures of gold and silver, or mixtures of these two metals, inlaid in the cast bronze blade. The Romans took up the technique with enthusiasm and used it not only for ambitious works but also for simpler objects, and from the first centuries of the Christian era there are innumerable specimens of this type of Roman art handicraft, from bronze statues and furniture to inkstands and pens.

In the Nordic territories incrustation appears as early as the first century B.C. Thus we sometimes find inlays of iron on the bows of bronze fibulae.

During the first centuries of the Christian era incrustation becomes increasingly common. Wires of silver are inlaid on bronze objects and jewels made of iron are given inlays of other metals. The spurs and spearheads of this Fig. xx a time are often decorated with inlaid lines, squared patterns or concentric rings in another metal. In domestic works the craftsmen as a rule confine themselves to simple patterns of this kind. Nevertheless the Nordic artist is well aware of the more complicated Roman technique, as is shown by a large number of beautifully incrusted works imported during this period into the Nordic lands.

During the Late Iron Age, that is to say from the 5th century until the 12th, incrustation is a common technique in Nordic art handicraft. Its popularity may have fallen off slightly during the three centuries between A.D. 500 and 800 – during which period, however, it had a brilliant flowering on the Continent – but during the Viking era it appears to have become popular once more. From the 9th, 10th and 11th centuries there is an abundance of incrusted Nordic art products, several of them of the very finest Fig. xx b class. The inlays occur particularly on weapons – spearheads and swords – but we also find them quite often on stirrups and other objects. Frequently the artist resorts to an interplay of several metals, such as silver, copper, bronze and brass, to form a lively pattern. Occasionally the inlaid wires are hammered out to form a layer covering the whole surface; in this overlay the artist engraves the pattern and fills in the lines with niello. Prominent parts of the decoration may be further accentuated by inlays of gold foils as on some of the more resplendent Nordic spearheads.

WILHELM HOLMQVIST

Filigree and Granulation

The term filigree comes from the Latin words *filum* = wire and *granum* = grain. In art metalwork, filigree is a widely spread technique which occurs either in pure form, i.e. with wires only, or with added grains. Decoration with grains only also occurs, and this is called granulation. Nowadays the terminological distinction between filigree and granulation is not very strictly observed and the common designation filigree is generally used.

The wires used in prehistoric filigree work are generally solid with a circular section, but they may also be semi-circular or even hollow, that is to say tubular. In addition there occur flat-hammered or flat-drawn wires as well as all conceivable modes of using these, such as twisting, plaiting, and so on. The wires may be beaded in different ways to produce an illusion of globular grains lying in a row, or they may be simply cross-hatched. Finer works can often be distinguished from simpler ones by the way in which the beading of the wires has been done. Thus there occur combinations of different wires looped, twisted, plaited, gathered in parallel lines, and so on.

In prehistoric times gold or silver wires were drawn in the same way as today, i.e. with dragpipes of iron or some other sufficiently resistant material, and the sections are often of different shapes and sizes according to the artist's needs. The grains for granulation could be made of a number of short pieces cut off from a wire and placed on a piece of charcoal or preferably on a layer of powdered charcoal. Exposed to heat, the pieces of gold melted and took a spherical form. When gold grains were being made on a larger scale the pieces of gold could be placed on powdered charcoal arranged in several layers separated from one another by plates. The whole could be put in a suitable vessel and heated up to the melting point of gold, after which it was cooled in water. The soldering of gold wires and the gold grains to the base is usually done with solder but the prehistoric craftsmen were so skilled that they are believed to have mastered other methods as well. One such method was as follows. When, for example, a gold grain is heated in charcoal until it is white-hot, its surface takes up so much carbon that it becomes dark and so has a *lower melting point than the normal value for gold*. Thus when the base is heated with the gold grains lying on it the latter will fuse to the base with the least possible contact surface. Afterwards the gold can again be heated up and then the remains of the dark surface – the gold carbide – will disappear altogether. The process is thus a kind of welding and the result is, as innumerable prehistoric jewels show, a light and vibrant surface decoration in which the individual gold grains seem to quiver as if they might roll away at the least breath or movement. – Another method is to fasten the wires and grains to the base with a special kind of glue. When then heated up they will fuse to the base without any other kind of solder.

The tools used in filigree work were tongs of different kinds, chisels, dragpipes and so on.

Historical Development

In the Mediterranean culture there was an early appreciation of the charm of the filigree and granulation appearing on an exquisite jewel or other art object. One such article which is often mentioned and illustrated is a dagger from the tomb of Tutankhamen, with a granulated handle. The Mycenaean graves and other Greek finds show examples of relatively sparse filigree and granulation, but it was not until the Etruscan culture that this type of art reached a peak which it never since regained. Well known here are the rows of running animals executed in dense granulation, or the chased animal friezes executed against a background filled with hundreds of glittering gold grains. Well known, too, are the chased face masks with beards and hair in granulation, the gold fibulae and brooches with granulation ornament of the most delicate kind. Etruscan art had its heyday in the 7th–5th centuries B.C., the period when its exquisite jewels were created, and it is certainly against this background that one should also regard the beautiful objects in gold and filigree which were still being manufactured during Hellenistic times.

Among the Romans, filigree work seems to have been less common. During the first centuries of the Christian era it would seem to have been more on the periphery of the Roman Empire than in its central parts that interest was shown in the technique, and perhaps it is for this reason that we precisely in contemporary Nordic art find outstanding specimens of the filigree art of this epoch.

A large gold neck ring found some years ago at Havor, Hablingbo parish, Gotland, may undoubtedly serve as a connecting link between the northeastern border states of the Roman Empire and the North at this period. This object is almost entirely in gold filigree with large chased terminal knobs decorated with bulls' heads and it presents a rich variety of granulation together with twisted and looped filigree wires of different kinds.

Whether this work is of domestic manufacture or not, it is undoubtedly closely connected with a large number of gold beads and berlocks found in the Nordic countries from the 2nd and 3rd centuries A.D. The majority of these objects were certainly made in these territories and they are extraordinarily beautiful specimens of Nordic gold filigree and granulation.

With these objects we are approaching to the heyday of Nordic filigree art, the 5th and 6th centuries A.D., when our art handicraft in this technique was unsurpassed of its kind. The most outstanding examples of this art are per-

Fig. XIV a, b

haps the gold collars of the 6th century, those resplendent jewels which would seem to have been intended for gods rather than men. Let us look at one of them. The figures which creep around between the richly articulated gold rings spun around with filigree take us to the world of sagas and trolls. The figures themselves are carved from small solid gold plates and are accentuated by filigree wires and gold grains so lightly welded to the surface that they seem to quiver. We discern birds, wild boars and dragons with flaring nostrils, serpents and sphinxes, and, in the midst of all this, face masks with staring eyes and human figures on bent legs and with their noses in the air. The filigree wires spun around are looped, twisted and plaited; they are beaded to the full extent; and, as if the artist was still not content with the effect he has laid actual gold grains in rows so that the light may play and be reflected at all angles. In other words we are in the presence of objects which are masterpieces of their kind and shining examples of Nordic art metalwork.

From the same epoch as the gold collars, i.e. the 5th and 6th centuries A.D., a quantity of gold filigree works Fig. XVI of the finest class are preserved in the Nordic territories. During the following era, the 7th and 8th centuries, the art of filigree is less prominent, although even then we find extremely fine works in both gold and silver. Subsequently, during the Viking era, there begins a new efflorescence which, under influences both from the Continent and from the British Isles, persists far into the Middle Ages. If we had to choose an epoch which was particularly Fig. VX, rich it would be the 10th and 11th centuries. The large VII a, b quantities of treasure finds from this period provide abundant evidence of the artistic achievements of the time. In contradistinction to the epoch of the gold collars, the leading metal of this period is silver, in which metal the artists succeed in producing filigree works which are little inferior to the filigree creations in the nobler metal. Nevertheless it is the gold works which are the finest of the period, and the important finds from Hon and Rød in Norway, from Hjortsberga and Ö. Vram in Sweden, from Hornelund and Frederiksborg in Denmark bear eloquent witness to this.

During the Viking era, in contrast to an earlier epoch, the artists begin increasingly to work with flat-hammered or flat-drawn wires which are either placed on edge on the base surface or twisted into a kind of spiral wire. This is equally common in gold and in silver. These wires may, of course, be either plaited or cross stamped. They may also have the edge furnished with a beaded wire or they may form part of combinations with beaded and twisted wires. Other innovations are also introduced.

WILHELM HOLMQVIST

Cloisonné

From time immemorial precious stones have been highly valued in goldsmiths' work. Often gems were credited with magical powers and then, as now, they were the most costly items used in goldsmithing. The prehistoric Nordic goldsmiths used only one kind of precious stone to any considerable extent – garnets. Garnets form the principal material in the magnificent polychrome inlays executed in cloisonné which adorn weapons and jewels from the Germanic Iron Age.

Figs. IX, XVIII, XIX

Cloisonné consists of flat-polished precious stones or enamel set in a system of metal cells (cloisons). The cells may often form a complicated pattern and the grinding and shaping of the stones was a process calling for great precision and skill. Cloisonné is an art of great antiquity: it was practised by the Sumerians and the Egyptians and later came to be a characteristic art form of the Scythian equestrian peoples in Asia. The Germanic peoples probably learned the art during the folk migrations when the Goths, among others, settled around the Black Sea, an area where, in cloisonné art, traditions from Scythian times had been preserved. The polychrome inlays appealed to the Germanic love of brilliant display and the cloisonné techique came to play a considerable and important part in Germanic goldsmiths' art.

The oldest technique used for setting in cloisonné in Germanic jewellery does not differ in principle from that used for free-standing inlays. The inlays are secured by pressing the upper part of the surrounding cell walls over them. The garnets used in this technique were usually very large and filled up practically the whole cell space. In order to give the object a certain flexibility, so that the garnets would not crack on being set, it was, however, usual to put a thin layer of resin in the bottom of the cell. The garnets in the oldest Germanic cloisonné works are distinguished by the extremely fine polishing they have received; the upper surface may be slightly convex, which adds to the brilliance of the gem. Yet another technique which was taken over from gem setting was that of placing a patterned gold or silver foil beneath the garnet, this too serving to enhance the lustre of the stone. The splendid sword pommel from Sturkö, made of solid gold Fig. XVIII with slightly arched garnets set in a strict geometrical pattern, is among the finest examples existing in the North of the oldest cloisonné technique. The pommel has been made with the same technique and is of the same high quality as the celebrated weapons from the tomb of the Merovingian king Childeric (d. A.D. 481). Each garnet has been individually cut with faceted edges and microscopic examination reveals that the characteristic stepped form was obtained with the aid of a file. On other works from the same period the surface of the garnets has an engraved ring which may be filled with gold or enamel, and we also have examples of relief-cut garnets in cloisonné inlays in the form of mussels or beaded pattern. Since classical times the file and the graver have been the characteristic instruments of the craftsmen who cut gems and cameos and it was probably in their workshops that cloisonné objects were originally made. When the art of cloisonné spread with the Germanic peoples over Western Europe, however, the techniques soon became simplified. In order to make the cutting of the garnets easier they were ground down to very thin plates and we find increasingly few examples of the surface having been engraved. The new technique, however, required that the goldsmiths' work should be filled up with cement. The cement might be of different types – plaster and clay were used – the principal function of the material being to fill up the work and to give it the same massive weight as the older gold cloisonné works. The garnets were still secured by pressing the tops of the cell walls over the edges of the stones, but the thick layer of cement meant that it was no longer necessary to solder the cell walls to the base with the same care as previously, as the cement kept the work stable. Because of this it was now possible to give greater variety to the cloisonné pattern. Whereas formerly the design of the cell system had been geometric, the pattern being repeated endlessly, the artists now also began to execute

Fig. 1
Foot of a brooch of bronze
with cloisonné inlays, in
the shape of a facial mask.
Sandegårda, Sanda parish,
Gotland. 7th cent. A.D.
Scale 2:1.

Germanic animal ornament in cloisonné. The development
from a geometric style to animal ornament in garnet cloisonné belongs to the Germanic art, but we find examples
of it both in Lombardic Italy and in Anglo-Saxon England,
in Friesland and in the Nordic territories, and it is not yet
possible to say in which area this advanced art began. In
its external form this type of garnet cloisonné recalls enamel work – especially contemporary Byzantian enamel work
– but its individuality lies in the fact that the artists have
succeeded in imposing a lively pattern of the hard gems.
Finds show that Northern Europe did not lag behind the
other areas in this art and it is there that we have the
Text figs. richest examples of the most advanced cloisonné technique
1, 2 of all where the cell walls are secured entirely by means of
cement. This cement no longer consists of clay or plaster
but is a mixture of finely crushed limestone and beeswax.
The mixture was heated, and in the resulting viscous fluid
the thin cell walls were set and the garnets pressed into
place. When the fluid was cooled it solidified and the garnets were held firm without it being necessary to press
the cell walls over the sides of the garnets. With this technique it was possible to make the cell walls thinner than
ever before, enabling the artist to embark on still richer
variations of design. But because it was no longer necessary to secure the garnets by bending over the cell walls,
the artists were no longer limited to soft metals such as
gold and silver. They began to make cloisonné inlays with
bronze walls and this speciality became particularly char-
Text acteristic of the North. Especially on Gotland there have
fig. 1 been found a very large number of button on bow brooches with cloisonné inlays of this type. It is interesting

Fig. 2
Side portion of a
pyramidal boss with animal
ornament in garnet
cloisonné. Gamla Uppsala,
Uppland. 7th cent. A.D.
Scale 4:1.

that although the artists tried to economize on precious
metals by using gilt bronze for jewels they always used
real garnets for the inlays. This may perhaps have been
due to the fact that it was possible to procure garnets from
near at hand; both in the Scandinavian mountain chains
and in Finnish Karelia there are deposits of high-quality
garnets which may have been used already in prehistoric
times. Of interest in this context are a pair of Gotlandic
button on bow brooches where a part of the inlays are of
green serpentine which may likewise have been derived
from deposits in the mountain chain.

The richest period for Nordic cloisonné is A.D. 400–800.
During the Viking era the art disappears altogether. As
early as the 8th century it is possible to observe a decline
in the skill applied to cloisonné inlays. The garnets no
longer have faceted edges but bear traces of having been
sawn only. The complicated stepped forms disappear altogether and the garnets are now arched or squarecut.
Nevertheless it is from this phase that there come some
of the most monumental cloisonné works ever manufactured in the Nordic regions, namely huge button on bow
brooches with a size of 30 cm. These brooches, which have
been found in northern Norway, central Sweden and Gotland, are not in a well preserved state because they were
largely based on cement, but originally they were doubtless
resplendent pieces. Perhaps are these objects – which must
have been ornaments to images of gods – a parallel to the
famous jewel of the nordic goddess Freyja, the so called
"Brisingamen", i.e. the "Flaming jewel". The gem garnet
has since classical times been regarded as a symbol of the
immortal love of gods and men and what stone could be
better suited to a Nordic goddess of love?
BIRGIT ARRHENIUS

Enamel

Fig. XXIII Enamel is a coloured glass flux which is fused to a metal-base. It consists of a silicate mixture – as a rule quartz sand which is mixed with soda and metallic oxides. The oxide serves as a colouring substance. The use of enamel is closely connected with the art of cloisonné. From early times the Egyptians and Sumerians used inlays of coloured glass which were fastened to the base with cement or were inset. The discovery of a way of fusing the coloured glass flux direct to the underlay is thought to have been made in Cyprus *c.* 1300 B.C., but it was not until about 500 B.C. that enamel began to be used more generally.

The Celts and Romans used enamel inlays to a very large extent and achieved great skill in this art. In Byzantian art, too, enamel played an important part.

Enamelling never occupied so important a place among the Germanic peoples as it did among the Celts and Romans, and when ever we find a developed enamelling art in the Germanic world it always seems to be in connection with Celtic or Roman influences. Thus from Anglo-Saxon England we know a number of very high-grade enamel works which have been developed more or less directly from Irish Celtic enamelling art, and the enamel inlays found among the Franks are probably connected with traditions preserved since Gallo-Roman times. During the Carolingian and Ottonian era enamelling in Europe experiences a new flowering which is probably attributable to Eastern influences.

In Nordic art enamel inlays are of comparatively minor importance. Here the inlays were made almost exclusively with garnets. With one or two exceptions the enamel inlays were carried out in the champlevé technique, i.e. the enamel was laid into more or less irregular pits in the metal. In the Nordic works the most commonly used enamel consists of a red or flame-coloured porous glass flux, obtained by adding iron oxide to the silicate mixture.

Whether the enamel is red or flame-coloured depends on oxidation level of the iron. The latter was easy to obtain; often in Sweden silicon in its natural state contains iron. The find of a crucible with red glass flux shows us also that this flux was produced in Sweden during the Germanic Iron Age. Particularly during the 7th century, red and flamecoloured beads in this type of coarse glass flux are very characteristic of the Nordic regions and their frequent occurrence is probably due to the fact that it is during this period that the coarse glass flux begins to be made in these regions to any considerable extent. It is from this period that the first definitely Nordic works with champlevé enamel are found. Red and flame-coloured enamel of this type was also used for enamel inlays on the bridle mounts from boat grave III at Vendel. These enamel Fig. XXIII inlays are in a technique related to cloisonné. Each enamel field is bounded by metal walls, the varying thickness of which gives the work a further decorative element. The enamel was secured to the base in the same way as in other Nordic works in champlevé technique, i.e. the surface of the metal base was roughened, after which the enamel was fused to it. The mounts from Vendel are among the finest enamel works encountered in the North. The view has been taken that it is an imported work, but finds of other mounts with enamel decoration indicate that this type of mount is a Nordic product. It is of interest that among the finds from Vendel there are also a number of very fine inlay works in garnet cloisonné. To a great extent Nordic enamelling seems to be complementary to garnet cloisonné, and it is not improbable that both these forms of decoration were executed in the same workshops. Like cloisonné, enamelling died out in the North during the early Viking era.

BIRGIT ARRHENIUS

Patination and Coloration

The colours of metals play an important part in goldsmiths' work and artists early learned how to create new
colour variations in the precious metals with the aid of
different metal alloys and chemical agents. Since Egyptian
times use had often been made of an alloy consisting of a
mixture of gold and silver, electrum. This had a pale gold-
en lustre, but with the aid of various chemicals it was
also possible to give the gold a reddish or greenish tinge.
By using on the same object gold with different alloys and
tones of colour the artist achieved rich polychrome effects.
Bronze and silver could also be varied with different patinas and during antiquity great experience in this art was
gained. Artists in the North seem to have taken over a
great deal of the classical knowledge in this sphere and
Nordic goldsmiths frequently used coloration and patination in order to achieve decorative effects.

Bronze, with its golden colour, was no doubt generally
used in unpatinated condition, but probably the artist also
knew how to use the different patinas of bronze from
leather brown to olive green.

During the late Viking era the bronzes often have a
brass-like colour which seems to be a deliberately produced patina.

Fig. IV For finer works bronze gilt was generally used. Fire gilding occurs in the North during the 4th century A.D. and
is thereafter used abundantly.

We know that the Romans performed fire gilding with
the aid of mercury – i.e. an amalgam of gold and mercury
was heated until the mercury volatilized and the gold was
left as a covering film. We have no clear evidence that
this type of gilding was used to a greater extent in the
North. Often we find on Nordic objects that verdigris
from the underlying bronze has penetrated through the
gilding and entirely covers it. This indicates that the gilding did not quite cover the object even though a
thick layer had been added. The reason may be that the

craftsmen used another gilding technique – one which was also used for pewtering (see below) and was employed until our own days in the gilding of porcelain. Under this technique powdered gold is mixed with a resinate – in prehistoric times this was probably liquid resin – to form a paste or size which was brushed on the object. When the latter was heated the resin was removed, leaving the gold, which after burnishing covered the surface. Fire gilding of this type is not difficult to perform and a comparatively thick layer can be achieved with this technique. The gilt is, however, very delicate and may easily be lost upon heating or upon contact with acids and salts. This is one of the reasons why bronzes gilded in prehistoric times are now, as a rule, in very poor condition.

Blanching, i.e. pewtering, is mentioned by the Roman writer Pliny who says that the Gauls discovered this method. Pewtering is very frequently found on provincial Roman works and was probably done in order to imitate silver. In the North we find it as early as the 2nd century A.D. The technique used was analogous to the second method described above, i.e. tin was mixed with liquid resin to form a size which was brushed on the object, which was then heated. At the same time as pewtering, use was made during Roman times of plating, i.e. the laying on of silver or gold foils which were welded to the base. During the late Germanic Iron Age plating becomes very rare in the Nordic material; it does not return on any large scale until the Viking era. Instead, pewtering dominates to an increasing extent and during the first part of the 7th century pewter seems to have driven out silver altogether as a metal for jewellery. During this phase one can also find pewtered objects which have been given a niello decoration, a type of ornament which in the North otherwise appears mainly on silver jewels.

Niello was used already by the Egyptians, and veritable masterpieces of this art have been found in the Mycenaean graves. In prehistoric times niello consisted as a rule of a mixture of copper and silver sulphur which was fused to the base by heat. True niello does not appear in the North until Roman times. However, even during the Bronze

Fig. XXIV

Fig. XVII a

Fig. XXII a, b

Age craftsmen achieved effects with the aid of resin inlays on bronze objects which in many ways remind one of niello. These inlays, intended to enhance the effect of engraved decoration, were applied in stamps, points or thin lines. In connection with the adoption by Nordic artists of provincial Roman stamped ornament, niello decoration found a rich use. During the Germanic Iron Age niello decoration had a more limited role, as it was then mainly used in the form of borders. Niello borders were used at first as a boundary for ornamented fields, but during the 7th century they are incorporated in animal ornaments, where raised mouldings with zig-zag decoration often constitute the internal decoration of the animals and follow the turns of the extremities like nerve threads. During the Viking era, with the more general use of silver plating, free niello decoration once more acquired greater importance. The artist now surrounded animal figures with niello or applied niello to the figures themselves either in the form of points or lines or as a complete covering.

The flowering of niello decoration during the Viking era has been associated with influences from Eastern Europe. Other features, however, show connections with West European art. Probably the same thing applies to niello decoration as to Nordic goldsmiths' art in general during the Viking era, where we find aboundant evidence of influences from both Eastern and Western Europe, all, however, blended into a genuine Nordic art with traditions firmly anchored in previous centuries.

The patination and coloration of metals call for a considerable knowledge of their chemical properties. The same kind of knowledge was also required in order to be able to carry out the quite complicated soldering operations with various alloys that were called for as the art of goldsmithing developed. The more one studies Nordic goldsmithing the more one is amazed by the skill with which the craftsman mastered these arts, in which complicated formulas must have been handed down by word of mouth.

BIRGIT ARRHENIUS

41

II
Cast silver brooch with gilt decoration. Vårby, Huddinge,
Södermanland. 10th cent. AD. Scale 1:1.

I (preceding page)
Cast bronze figure. Rällinge, Lunda, Södermanland.
11th cent. AD. Scale 4:1.

III a
Sword pommel with mould-stamped, cast and engraved
decoration. Ihre, Hellvi, Gotland. C. 800 AD.
Scale approx. 1:1.

b
Bronze mount with cast decoration. Ulfsunda, Stockholm.
9th cent. AD. Scale 3:1.

IV (opposite page)
Bronze-gilt mount with cast,
stamped and engraved decoration. Broa, Halla, Gotland.
8th cent. AD. Scale 4:1.

V
Shield mount of bronze gilt
with animal ornament; en-
graved border of silver with
niello inlays. Nabberör, Böda,
Öland. 8th cent. AD .Scale 2:1.

VI

Bronze-gilt vane with pierced and engraved decoration. Söderala church, Hälsingland. 11th cent. AD. Scale 1:3.

VII a
Chased fluted bowl with gilded and engraved rim. Lilla
Valla, Rute, Gotland. 11th cent. AD. Scale 1:2.

b
Detail of shield handle with silver bosses granulation and
inlaid blue stones. Brostorp, Glömminge, Öland,
2nd cent. AD. Scale 1:1,

VIII
Mount of knife-sheath of
bronze, originally gilded,
with cast and engraved
decoration. Bjers, Hejnum,
Gotland. 8th cent. AD.
Scale 3:2.

IX (opposite page)
Belt-end mount of bronze gilt
with cast and engraved
decoration (chip carving),
inlays of garnets and niello.
Vendel, Uppland. 7th cent. AD.
Scale 4:1.

X
Silver-gilt brooch with cast
and engraved decoration,
mouldings inlaid with niello.
Svennevad, Närke. 6th cent. AD.
Scale 3:2.

XI (opposite page)
Detail of gold bracteate
with die-stamped central
image and stamped border,
filigree decoration and
sculptured face masks.
Gerete, Fardhem, Gotland.
6th cent. AD. Scale 2:1.

XII
Bronze matrices for pressed
foils, cast with carved
details. Björnhovda,
Torslunda, Öland. 7th cent. AD.
Scale 1:1.

XIII
Solid gold neck rings with
stamped decoration, from
different find places.
5th-6th cents. AD. Scale 1:1.

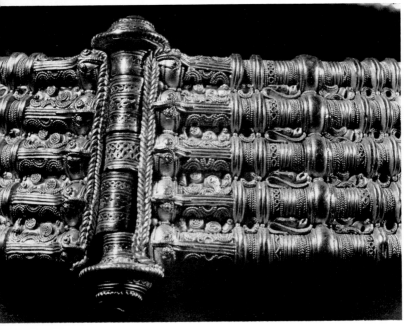

XIV
Details of 3- and 5-ringed gold collars with filigree, granulation and carved figures. Ålleberg, Västergötland and Färjestaden, Öland. 6th cent. AD. Scale 2:1.

XV
Detail of gold bracteate with die-stamped central image and stamped borders; filigree decoration and sculptured face masks. Åsum, Skåne. 6th cent. AD. Scale 2:1.

XVI a b
Gold mounts for sword scabbards, with filigree and granulation
on a solid carved base. Tureholm, V. Ljung, Södermanland.
6th cent. AD. Scale 5:3.

XX a
Spur of iron with
silver incrustation
and silver filigree.
Hörninge, Köping,
Öland. 2nd cent. AD.
Scale 3:2.

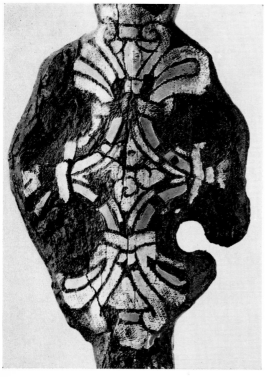

b
Detail of spearhead
with gold and silver
incrustation. Klinte,
Follingbo, Gotland.
11th cent. AD.
Scale 4:3.

XXI a
Pressed foil of silver gilt for a drinking vessel. Lilla Jored,
Kville, Bohuslän. 4th cent. AD. Scale 3:2.

b
Mount of bronze gilt, cast and engraved, and pewter inlaid
with niello. Vendel, Uppland. 7th cent. AD. Scale 2:1.

XXII a
Ring brooch of silver-plated bronze with figures in niello,
applied gold foils with filigree and granulation. Austris,
Tingstäde, Gotland. 10th cent. AD. Scale 4:3.

b
Ring brooch of bronze gilt, silver-plated ridges with niello.
Birka, Uppland. 10th cent. AD. Scale 1:1.

XXIII
Bridle mounts of bronze gilt with enamel inlays of red and
flame-coloured glass flux. Vendel, Uppland. 8th cent. AD.
Scale 1:2.

XXIV (following page)
Female figure in bronze gilt, cloak with pewter overlay.
Tuna, Alsike, Uppland. 8th cent. AD. Scale 6:1.

Catalogue

Golden Age and Viking Art in Sweden

1 CRUCIBLES, hard fired, vitrified surface, for melting precious metals. – Helgö, Ekerö, Uppland.

2 MOLD, sandstone, for casting metal bars. – Svarta Jorden, Birka, Uppland.
BRONZE BAR. – Helgö, Ekerö, Uppland.

3 MOLD, sandstone, for casting a round pendant. Viking period. – Svarta Jorden, Birka, Uppland.

4 MOLD, unfinished, sandstone, with engraved circular figures. Viking period. – Svarta Jorden, Birka, Uppland.

5 MOLDS, fragments, fired fine-grained clay. – Helgö, Ekerö, Uppland.

6 MOLDS, fragments, fired, fine-grained clay, for casting tortoise brooches. Viking period. – Svarta Jorden, Birka, Uppland.

7 MOLD, fragment, fired, fine-grained clay for casting an ornamental pin. Viking period. – Svarta Jorden, Birka, Uppland.

8 MOLD, fragment, fired, fine-grained clay. – Svarta Jorden, Birka, Uppland.

9 MOLD, fired, fine-grained clay. 8th century A.D. – Helgö, Ekerö, Uppland.

10 MOLD, fired, fine-grained clay. – Helgö, Ekerö, Uppland.

11 MOLD, fragment, fired, fine-grained clay. – Helgö, Ekerö, Uppland.
CONICAL BRONZE PIECES (from a mold). – Helgö, Ekerö, Uppland.

12 MOLD, fired, fine-grained clay, for casting a brooch. 7th century A.D. – Helgö, Ekerö, Uppland.
BROOCH, bronze, molded, with inlays of mother-of-pearl. 7th century A.D. – Harby, Ljungby, Småland.

13 MOLD, fragment, fired, fine-grained clay, for casting a chape. Viking period. – Svarta Jorden, Birka, Uppland.
CHAPE, bronze, open work. Ring impressions made in the mold. – Åstad, Långlöt, Öland.

14 MOLD, fragment, fired, fine-grained clay, for casting a clasp button, 6th century A.D. – Helgö, Ekerö, Uppland.
CLASP button gilded bronze, inlaid with niello. Compare adjacent mold. 6th century A.D. – Nicktuna, Tortuna, Västmanland.

15 MOLD, fired, fine-grained clay, for casting a brooch. 6th century A.D. – Helgö, Ekerö, Uppland.

Brooch, bronze. Compare adjacent mold. 6th century A.D. – Helgö, Ekerö, Uppland.

16 Mold, soapstone, for casting an ornamental pin. Viking period. – Svarta Jorden, Birka, Uppland.

17 Modern wax model for making a tortoise brooch. Modern reconstruction of molds for the above. Tortoise brooches, bronze. – Åshusby, Norrsunda, Uppland.

18 Brooches, gilded bronze, casting repeated and each specimen then engraved with essentially the same decorations, small details differing. 6th century A.D. – Bjällsta, Indal, Medelpad; Sörfors, Attmar, Medelpad; Hade, Hedesunda, Gästrikland.

19 Clasp buttons, gilded silver, several from the same mold, inlaid with niello. 6th century A.D. – Hult, Ånimskog, Dalsland.

20 Clasp buttons, gilded bronze, several from the same mold. 5th century A.D. – Brucebo, Väskinde, Gotland.

21 Brooch, bronze, in the form of a quadruped, cast, with stamped decorations. 6th century A.D. – Unknown provenance, Gotland.

22 Brooch, as above. 5th century A.D. – Bjärge, Vallstena, Gotland.

23 Brooches, bronze, cast. 11th century A.D. – Annexet, Hemse, Gotland.

24 Belt mountings, bronze, cast decorations. 9th century A.D. – Ulfsunda, Bromma, Stockholm.

25 Brooch, bronze, cast, with stamped decorations. 6th century A.D. – Lenstad, Torslunda, Öland.

26 brooch, three-lobed, silver, cast, partly gilded, with niello and gold inlay. 10th century A.D. – Östra Herrestad, Skåne.

27 Animal head, gilded bronze, cast. 10th–11th century A.D. – Unknown provenance.

28 Bracelet, silver, cast. Viking period. – Ivö, Skåne.

29 Rings, bronze, cast, with bud-like protuberances. 5th–6th century A.D. – Unknown provenance, Öland. Rings, see above. – Unknown provenance, Öland.

30 Strap end, bronze, cast, with facial mask. 5th century A.D. – Väsby, Ekerö, Uppland.

31 Bracelet, bronze, cast decorations. Viking period. – Bolmsö, Småland.

32 Tongue-shaped brooches, bronze, several from the same mold 10th century A.D. – Birka, Uppland; Frösöläger, Jämtland.

33 Clasps, gilded silver, several made from the same mold and then engraved. 6th century A.D. – Grumpan, Sävare, Västergötland.

34 Mountings, gilded bronze, probably cast decorations but then improved by engraving. 8th century A.D. – Vendel, Uppland.

35 Tortoise brooches, bronze, partly gilded, with cast animal figures attached, impressions of textile underneath. 10th century A.D. – Unknown provenance, Öland.

36 HUMAN FIGURE, fertility god, bronze, cast. 11th century A.D. – Rällinge, Lunda, Södermanland.

37 BROOCH, silver, originally gilded, cast and then considerably improved by engraving, details in niello. 10th century A.D. – Jämjö, Gärdslösa, Öland.

38 BROOCH, gilded silver, cast and then engraved. 10th century A.D. – Vårby, Huddinge, Södermanland.

39 BROOCH, like No. 37 above.

40 BROOCH, silver, cast, with cast animal figures attached. 10th century A.D. – Torsta, Tuna, Hälsingland.

41 BROOCH, like No. 40 above. 10th century A.D. – Ekeskog, Hejde, Gotland.

42 BRACELET, gold, two twisted rods. 11th century A.D. – Erikstorp, Ödeshög, Östergötland.

43 NECKLACE, gold, twisted rod. 3rd–4th century A.D. – Vackerby, Frustuna, Södermanland.

44 BRACELET, gold, two twisted rods. 11th century A.D. – Kullingbos, Källunge, Gotland.

45 NECKLACE, silver, twisted rods in pairs, stamped impressions. 11th century A.D. – Kyrkobyn, Grönby, Skåne.

46 NECKLACE, silver, three twisted rods and intertwined threads, stamped impressions. 10th–11th century A.D. – Unknown provenance.

47 NECKLACE, silver, like No. 46 above. 10th–11th century A.D. – Unknown provenance, Gotland.

48 BRACELET, silver, two twisted rods. 10th–11th century A.D. – Lindarve, Ekeby, Gotland.

49 BRACELET, in spiral, silver, rifled rods, 9th–10th century A.D. – Asarve, Hemse, Gotland.

50 NECKLACE, silver, three pairs of twisted rods. 10th–11th century A.D. – Skarpa Alby, Sandby, Öland.

51 NECKLACE, silver, three pairs of twisted rods and intertwined, twisted thread. 10th–11th century A.D. – Unknown provenance.

52 BRACELET, silver, two pairs of twisted rods and intertwined, twisted threads. 10th–11th century A.D. – Unknown provenance.

53 BRACELET, hammered silver. – 10th–11th century A.D. – Liknatte, Stenkyrka, Gotland.

54 BROOCH, gilded silver, cast and then engraved. Details with niello and garnets in cells. 6th century A.D. – När, Gotland.

55 BROOCH, like No. 54 above. 6th century A.D. – Unknown provenance. Öland.

56 BROOCH, gilded silver, made like 54 and 55 above. 6th century A.D. – Svennevad, Närke.

57 BROOCH, gilded silver, made like No. 56 above. 6th century A.D. – Ekeby, Uppland.

58 BRIDLE MOUNTINGS, gilded bronze, cast and then engraved (chip carving). Edged in white, nielloed metal. 7th century A.D. – Vendel, Uppland.

59 SHIELD MOUNTINGS, gilded bronze, cast and then engraved. Edged in silver, engraved and nielloed. 8th century A.D. – Nabberör, Böda, Öland.

60 BRIDLE MOUNTINGS, gilded bronze, cast and then engraved and stamped. Latter part of the 8th century A.D. – Broa, Halla, Gotland.

61 SWORD POMMEL, gilded silver, cast and then engraved and nielloed. 6th century A.D. – Grimeton, Halland.

62 SWORD SHEATH MOUNTINGS, bronze, cast and then engraved, partly gilded and engraved decorations. 650–750 A.D. – Bjers, Hejnum, Gotland.

63 WEATHER VANE, gilded bronze, open work, engraved and stamped decorations. Latter part of the 11th century A.D. – Söderala, Hälsingland.

64 SHIELD BOSS, iron, with plated bronze sheets in repoussé. 7th century A.D. – Ultuna, Bondkyrka, Uppland.

65 PRESS MODEL for repoussé work, bronze. 10th century A.D. – Sigtuna, Uppland.

66 PRESS MODELS for repoussé work, bronze. 7th century A.D. – Björnhovda, Torslunda, Öland.

67 GOLD RINGS, chased, with engraved details. 5th–6th century A.D. – Mörby, Löt, Öland; Spångebro, Löt, Öland; Traneberg, Gestad, Dalsland.

68 BEAD, silver, chased, with filigrée. 10th century A.D. – Ytings, Othem, Gotland.
BEAD as above. – Petes, Öja, Gotland.

69 SHIELD HANDLE, bronze, partly silver plated, filigrée, granulation and inlaid blue stones, the spherical heads of the rivets are covered with hammered silver sheets. 2nd century A.D. – Brostorp, Glömminge, Öland.

70 REPOUSSÉ WORK, gilded silver. 3rd–4th century A.D. – Lilla Jored, Kville, Bohuslän.

71 GOLD SHEETS in repoussé with human figures. 7th century(?) A.D. – Bolmsö, Småland.
Gold sheet in repoussé with human figure. 6th century A.D. – Ravlunda, Skåne.

72 GOLD SHEETS in repoussé with human figures. 8th–9th century A.D. – Helgö, Ekerö, Uppland.

73 SILVER BOWL, chased, partly gilded and engraved. 11th century A.D. – Lilla Valla, Rute, Gotland.

74 GOLD BANDS for cloisonné work. 7th century A. D. – Tuna, Väte, Gotland.
GARNETS for cloisonné work. 8th century A.D. – Helgö, Ekerö, Uppland.

75 SWORD POMMEL, gold, with garnets in cloisonné. The end of the 5th century A.D. – Sturkö, Blekinge.

76 GOLD SHEET for sword pommel in cloisonné. 7th century A.D. – Gamla Uppsala, Uppland.

77 SWORD POMMEL, gold with garnets in cloisonné. 7th century A.D. – Skräfsta, Botkyrka, Uppland.

78 SWORD POMMEL, like No. 77 above. 550–650 A.D. – Edsten, Hög, Kville, Bohuslän.

79 PART OF SWORD HANDLE, gilded bronze, the pommel with garnets in gold cloisonné, details of twisted and beaded gold filigrée threads. 550–650 A.D. – Vallstenarum, Gotland.

80 BUCKLE, gilded silver, cast and then engraved, with garnets in gold cloisonné. 550–650 A.D. – Tuna, Alsike, Uppland.

81 BROOCH, silver, with plated silver sheets, partly imitation filigrée, inlaid blue stone. 4th century A.D. – Havor, Hablingbo, Gotland.

82 BROOCH, silver, like No. 81 above. 4th century A.D. – Kabbarp, Tottarp, Skåne.

83 BROOCH, gilded bronze, cast, with stamped decorations and garnets, cloisonné, and mother-of-pearl. 7th century A.D. – Endregårda, Endre, Gotland.

84 BROOCH, gilded bronze, like No. 83 above. 7th century A.D. – Kylver, Stånga, Gotland.

85 BROOCH, gilded bronze, like No. 83 above. 7th century A.D. – Bjers, Hejnum, Gotland.

86 BROOCH, gilded bronze, like No. 83 above. 600–650 A.D. – Ihre, Hellvi, Gotland.

87 BROOCH, gilded bronze, like No. 83 above. 7th century A.D. – Grötlingbo, Gotland.

88 BROOCH, gilded bronze, like No. 83 above. – Vallstenarum, Vallstena, Gotland.

89 BROOCH, gilded bronze, like No. 83 above. 7th century A.D. – Grötlingbo, Gotland.

90 BROOCH, gilded bronze, like No. 83 above. 7th century A.D. – Unknown provenance, Gotland.

91 BROOCH, gilded bronze, like No. 83 above, inlaid serpentine stone. 7th century A.D. – Alands, Hogrän, Gotland.

92 BROOCH, gilded bronze, like No. 83 above. About 600 A.D. – Lilla Bjärges, Lau, Gotland.

93 BROOCH, gilded bronze, like No. 83 above. About 600 A.D. – Hejnum, Gotland.

94 BROOCH, gilded bronze, like No. 83 above, inlaid serpentine stone. About 600 A.D. – Bjers, Hejnum, Gotland.

95 BROOCH, bronze, like No. 83 above. 550–600 A.D. – Hade, Hedesunda, Gästrikland.

96 BROOCH, bronze, like No. 83 above, inlaid with yellow-white serpentine stone and blue, opaque glass. About 600 A.D. – Sandegårda, Sanda, Gotland.

97 BROOCH, gilded silver, like No. 83 above. 550–600 A.D. – Trull-halsar, Anga, Gotland.

98 BROOCH, bronze, like No. 83 above, 7th century A.D. – Roes, Grötlingbo, Gotland.

99 STRAP END, gilded bronze, cast and engraved, with garnets in cloisonné. About 650 A.D. – Vendel, Uppland.

100 CHAIN DIVIDER, bronze, cast and engraved, with garnets in cloisonné. About 700 A.D. – Kunsta, Adelsö, Uppland.

101 BRIDLE MOUNTINGS, gilded bronze, cast, inlaid with red and reddish-yellow enamel. 8th century A.D. – Vendel, Uppland.

102 SHIELD HANDLE, gilded bronze, cast, inlaid with red enamel. 8th century A.D. – Lackalänga, Skåne.

103 BEADS, red and reddish-yellow enamel. 7th century A.D. – Harby, Ljungby, Småland.

104 Pieces of red and reddish-yellow enamel. – Svenskens, Endre, Gotland.

105 BICONICAL BEADS, gold, with filigrée and granulation. The two biggest ones have bull's heads soldered on the surface. 2nd century A.D.

106 PENDANT, gold, with filigrée and granulation. 2nd century A.D. – Hallestorp, Vårkumla, Västergötland.

107 PENDANT, gold, like No. 106 above. – Lerkaka, Runsten, Öland.

108 PENDANT, gold, like No. 106 above. – Hörninge, Köping, Öland.

109 NECKLACE, gold, with chased end knobs, filigrée and granulation and with carved bulls' heads soldered on the surface. 1st–2nd century A.D. – Havor, Hablingbo, Gotland.

110 COLLAR, gold, with filigrée and granulation and with carved human and animal figures. 6th century A.D. – Ålleberg, Väster-götland.

111 COLLAR, gold, with filigrée and granulation and with carved animal figures. 6th century A.D. – Färjestaden, Torslunda, Öland.

112 FINGER RING, gold, hammered, engraved and with filigrée. 3rd–4th century A.D. – Ekeryd, Byarum, Småland.

113 SWORD POMMEL, gold. Soldered on a frame work are carved animal figures in open work. The animal figures are accentuated with filigrée and granulation. 6th century A.D. – Skurup, Skåne.

114 SCABBARD MOUNTS, gold, like No. 113 above. 6th century A.D. – Tureholm, Västerljung, Södermanland.

115 CARVED HUMAN AND ANIMAL FIGURES, gold, with filigrée, belonging to collar 110.

116 NODES TO A COLLAR?, gold, hammered, engraved. – Trollhättan, Västergötland.

117 PENDANT, gold, with filigrée and granulation. 10th–11th century A.D. – Botvatte, Ala, Gotland.

118 THORS HAMMER, silver, on the front side inlaid gilded silver sheets, adorned with filigrée in gold (on the back filigrée in

silver). 11th century A.D. – Erikstorp, Ödeshög, Östergötland.

119 BROCH, silver with a silver sheet in repoussé and adorned with filigrée and granulation. 10th–11th century A.D. – Unknown provenance, Södermanland?.

120 PENDANT, gold, with filigrée and granulation. 10th–11th century A.D. – Store Enbjenne, Hogrän, Gotland.

121 PENDANT, gold, like No. 120 above. 11th century A.D. – Lacka-länga, Skåne.

122 PENDANT, gold, like No. 120 above. 10th–11th century A.D. – Malms myr, Rone, Gotland.

123 PENDANT, gold, like No. 120 above. 10th–11th century A.D. – Malms myr, Rone, Gotland.

124 BEADS, gold and silver, with filigrée and granulation. 11th century A.D.

125 BOX-SHAPED BROOCH, bronze, with silverplated, engraved and nielloed edging, twisted silver wires and gold sheets in repoussé, adorned with filigrée and granulation. 11th century A.D. – Mårtens, Grötlingbo, Gotland.

126 GOLDS SHEETS, in repoussé with filigrée and granulation. 11th century A.D. – Malms myr, Rone, Gotland.

127 NECKLACE, gold, hammered and with stamped decorations. 3rd–4th century A.D. – Höviksnäs, Valla, Bohuslän.

128 NECKLACE, gold, hammered and with engraved and stamped decorations. 6th century A.D. – Tollesrud, Värmskog, Värmland.

129 NECKLACE, gold, like No. 128 above. – Bragnum, Floby, Väster-götland.

130 BRACELET, gold, hammered and with engraved and stamped decorations. Hanging on the bracelet are 4 spiral rings and a finger ring. 5th–6th century A.D. – Hässelby, Algutsrum, Öland.

131 BRACELET, gold, hammered and with stamped decorations. 3rd–4th century A. D. – Hede, Möklinta, Västmanland.

132 FINGER RING, gold, hammered and with stamped decorations. 4th century A.D. – Stora Brattön, Solberga, Bohuslän.

133 FINGER RING, gold, hammered and with engraved decorations. Viking period. – Kullingbos, Källunge, Gotland.

134 FINGER RING, gold, like No. 133 above.

135 BRACELET, gold, hammared and with engraved and stamped decorations. 3rd century A.D. – Tuna, Hjälsta, Uppland.

136 BRACELET, gold, like No. 135 above. – Bredinge, Kastlösa, Öland.

137 BRACTEATE, gold, stamped decorations. Under the loop are carved face-masks and filigrée. 6th century A.D. – Gerete, Fardhem, Gotland.

138 BRACTEATE, gold, like No. 137 above. 6th century A.D. – Åsum, Skåne.

139 BRACTEATE, gold, like No. 137 above. 6th century A.D. – Rav-lunda, Skåne.

51

140 BRACTEATE, gold, stamped decorations and filigrée. 6th century A.D. – Tossene, Bohuslän.

141 BRACTEATE, gold, stamped decorations. 6th century A.D. – Söderby, Danmark, Uppland.

142 BRACTEATE, gold, stamped decorations and filigrée. 7th–8th century A.D. – Norrgårda, Björke, Gotland.

143 BRACTEATE, gold, like No. 142 above. – Kodings, Hemse, Gotland.

144 BRACTEATE, silver stamped decorations. 7th–8th century A.D. – Fleringe, Gotland.

145 BRACTEATE, silver, like No. 144 above. – Dalhem, Gotland.

146 BRACTEATE, gold, like No. 144 above. – Norrgårda, Björke, Gotland.

147 BRACTEATE, silver, like No. 145 above.

148 BRACTEATE, silver, like No. 145 above.

149 BRACTEATE, silver, like No. 145 above.

150 DETAILS OF A SWORD HILT, bronze, cast in a mold with stamped impressions. About 800 A.D. – Ihre, Hellvi, Gotland.

151 BROOCH, gilded bronze, cast in a mold with stamped impressions, then engraved; originally adorned with garnets in cloisonné. 8th century A.D. – Othem, Gotland.

152 BRACELETS, silver, hammered, and with stamped decorations. 3rd century A.D. – Valla, Klinte, Gotland.

153 PENANNULAR BROOCH, silver, hammered and with stamped decorations. 11th century A.D. – Västergården, Fide, Gotland.

154 PENANNULAR BROOCH, silver, like No. 153 above. – Sutarve, Kräklingbo, Gotland.

155 PENANNULAR BROOCH, silver, like No. 153 above. 10th–11th century A.D. – Sigsarve, Hejde, Gotland.

156 PENANNULAR BROOCH, silver, like No. 153 above. 10th–11th century A.D. – Sigsarve, Hejde, Gotland.

157 PENANNULAR BROOCH, silver, like No. 153 above. – Vestrume, Rute, Gotland.

158 PENANNULAR BROOCH, silver, like No. 153 above. – Sutarve, Kräklingbo, Gotland.

159 PENANNULAR BROOCH, silver, like No. 153 above. – Koparve, Grötlingbo, Gotland.

160 FINGER RING, silver, hammered and with stamped decorations 10th–11th century A.D. – Barshaga, Othem, Gotland.

161 BRACELET, silver, hammered and with stamped decorations. 10th century A.D. – Hejdeby, Gotland.

162 BRACELET, silver, like No. 161 above. 10th–11th century A.D. – Laxarve, Boge, Gotland.

163 BRACELET, silver, like No. 161 above. – Vamlingbo or Sundre, Gotland.

164 BRACELET, silver, like No. 161 above. – Lindarve, Ekeby, Gotland.

165 BRACELET, silver, like 161 above. – Liknatte, Stenkyrka, Gotland.

166 BRACELET, silver, like No. 161 above. – Barshaga, Othem, Gotland.

167 BRACELET, silver, like No. 161 above. – Laxarve, Boge, Gotland.

168 BRACELET, silver, like No. 161 above. – Unknown provenance, Gotland.

169 BRACELET, silver, like No. 161 above. – Liknatte, Stenkyrka, Gotland.

170 STRAP-END, bronze, cast. About 100 A.D.
STRAP-END, bronze, with the patina removed. About 100 A.D. – Unknown provenance, Gotland.

171 BROOCHES, buckle and bridle mount, bronze, cast, with engraved decorations. Patina removed. 5th century A.D. – Lilla Bjärges, Lau, Gotland.

172 BELT RING, bronze, cast. Patina removed. About the beginning of the Christian Era. – Unknown provenance.

173 BROOCH, bronze, cast, engraved. Patina removed. 5th century A.D. – Unknown provenance.

174 HORSE BIT, iron and bronze, the iron rings inlaid with bronze. Patina removed. 5th century A.D. – Unknown provenance.

175 BROOCH, bird-shaped, bronze, cast and engraved, white metal-plated. 7th century A.D. – Unknown provenance, Öland.

176 BROOCH, bronze, like No. 175 above. 7th century A.D. – Södra Möckleby, Öland.

177 STRAP-END, bronze, cast, gilded. 9th century A.D. – Helgö, Ekerö, Uppland.

178 PENDANT, wheel-shaped, silver, cast, gilded and nielloed. 10th century A.D. – Unknown provenance, Skåne.

179 FEMALE FIGURE, bronze, cast, engraved, partly gilded and white metal-plated. 8th century A.D. – Tuna, Alsike, Uppland.

180 FINGER RING, gold, with silvercontent, hammered. 5th century A.D. – Helgö, Ekerö, Uppland.

181 PENDANT, bronze, open work, cast, stamped, gilded and white metal-plated. 8th century A.D. – Tuna, Alsike, Uppland.

182 DRESS PINS, bronze, cast, gilded. 11th century A.D. – Kyrkogården, Endre, Gotland.

183 TORTOISE BROOCH, bronze, cast, gilded and white metal-plated; details adorned with silver threads. 10th century A.D. – Unknown provenance, Öland.

184 BROOCH, bronze, gilded, engraved and white metal-plated. 7th century A.D. – Unknown provenance, Öland.

185 S-SHAPED BROOCH, bronze, cast, stamped. 550–600 A.D. – Torslunda, Öland.

186 CLASP BUTTON, bronze, cast, and nielloed, gilding removed. 6th century A.D. – Väsby, Ekerö, Uppland.

187 CLASP BUTTON, bronze, cast, gilded and nielloed: 6th century A.D. – Havor, Hablingbo, Gotland.

53

188 PENDANT, gilded bronze, cast, stamped. 8th century A.D. – Tuna, Alsike, Uppland.

189 DETAIL OF A BROOCH (the back side), bronze, cast in a mold with stamped impressions, engraved, partly gilded and white metal-plated. Viking period. – Unsarve, Halla, Gotland.

190 STRAP DIVIDER, bronze, cast, partly gilded, white metal-plated, stamped edgings. 7th century A.D. – Vallsrum, Runsten, Öland.

191 BROOCH, open work, cast, stamped and white metal-plated. 7th century A.D. – Harby, Ljungby, Småland.

192 BROOCH, silver, cast, gilded and nielloed. 11th century A.D. – Gerete, Fardhem, Gotland.

193 BROOCH, bronze, cast, silver-plated, stamped, and granulated. 2nd century A.D. – Roes, Rone, Gotland.

194 BROOCH, bronze, cast, partly silver-plated and gilded, stamped decorations. 5th century A.D. – Målartorp, Räpplinge, Öland.

195 BROOCH, bronze, cast, plated with stamped gold sheets. 2nd century A.D. – Varnhem, Västergötland.

196 BROOCH, bronze, cast, partly silver-plated and with filigrée and granulation. 2nd century A.D. – Unknown provenance.

197 STRAP-END, bronze, cast, silver-plated, stamped. 4th century A.D. – Broa, Halla, Gotland.

198 BRIDLE MOUNTING, bronze, silver-plated, partly gilded, stamped. 5th century A.D. – Roasjö, Västergötland.

199 MOUNTING FOR A SWORD HILT, silver, gilded, engraved and nielloed. 5th century A.D. – Djurgårdsäng, Skara, Västergötland.

200 BELT MOUNTING, silver, cast and then engraved, gilded, stamped and nielloed. 5th century A.D. – Sjörup, Häglinge, Skåne.
BORDER, silver, engraved and nielloed. 5th century A.D. – Sjörup, Häglinge, Skåne.

201 BROOCH, silver, partly gilded, stamped and nielloed in crossing lines. 5the century A.D. – Bostorp, Norra Möckleby, Öland.

202 THREE-LOBED BROOCH, bronze, cast and then engraved, engravings filled with niello. 10th century A.D. – Sövestad, Skåne.

203 PENDANT, bronze, cast, silver-plated, partly gilded, engraved and nielloed. 11th century A.D. – Broa, Halla, Gotland.

204 BEAD DIVIDER, bronze, cast, silver-plated, partly gilded, engraved and nielloed. 11th century A.D. – Myrände, Atlingbo, Gotland.

205 BROOCH, bronze, cast, gilded, silver-plated details originally nielloed. 11th century A.D. – Annexet, Hemse, Gotland.

206 BROOCH, bronze, cast, gilded, silver-plated details, nielloed, adorned with silver threads. 11th century A.D. – Slitehamn, Othem, Gotland.

207 PENANNULAR BROOCH, bronze, gilded, silver-plated and nielloed details. 10th century A.D. – Birka, Uppland.

208 PENANNULAR BROOCH, bronze, silver-plated, gilded details, nielloed, stamped gold sheets with filigrée and granulation. 10th–11th century A.D. – Austris, Tingstäde, Gotland.

209 BROOCH, bronze, cast, gilded, silver-plated details, nielloed, stamped gold sheets with filigrée. 11th century A.D. – Pilgårds, Boge, Gotland.

210 STRAP DIVIDER, bronze, cast, gilded and then engraved, white metal-plated, nielloed. 7th century A.D. – Vendel, Uppland.

211 BROOCH, bronze, cast, gilded, silver-plated and nielloed details. 11th century A.D. – Hellinge, Sjonhem, Gotland.

212 SPUR, iron, inlaid with silver and bronze. 3rd century A.D. – Endregårda, Endre, Gotland.

213 SPUR, bronze, inlaid with silver. 2nd century A.D. – Hemse, Gotland.

214 SPUR, bronze and iron, inlaid with silver, silver filigrée. 2nd century A.D. – Hörninge, Köpıng, Öland.

215 SPUR, bronze and iron, inlaid with copper. 2nd century A.D. – Endregårda, Endre, Gotland.

216 BUCKLE, iron, inlaid with bronze. 2nd century A.D. – Bläsungs, Väskinde, Gotland.

217 BELT MOUNTING, iron, inlaid with bronze. 550–650 A.D. – Gamla Uppsala, Uppland.

218 SADDLE MOUNTING, bronze, silver-plated, inlaid with silver, stamped details. 5th century A.D. – Vennebo, Roasjö, Västergötland.

219 SPEAR HEAD, iron, inlaid with silver forming an even surface where the decorations are lightly engraved. Unfinished work. 11th century A.D. – Lokrume, Gotland.

220 SWORD, iron handle inlaid with silver, copper and brass (galmeja). 9th century A.D. – Broa, Halla, Gotland.

221 SPEAR HEAD, iron, inlaid with gold and silver. Engraved lines inlaid with niello. 11th century A.D. – Klinte, Follingbo, Gotland.

222 SPEAR HEAD, iron, inlaid with silver, bronze and copper. 9th–10th century A.D. – Häggvik, Sollentuna, Uppland.

223 BRONZE BARS. – Stora Enbjenne, Hogrän, Gotland.

224 SILVER BARS. – Djurgårdsäng, Skara, Västergötland.

225 GOLD BARS, the weight corresponds to 143 gold solidi. – Storegården, Skarstad, Västergötland.

226 GOLD BAR, the weight corresponds to 225 gold solidi. – Timboholm, Skövde, Västergötland.

227 BRACELET, gold, the weight corresponds to 40 gold solidi. – Lilla Ryftes, Fole, Gotland.

228 RODS, gold, the weight corresponds to 196 gold solidi. – Jettened, Gudhem, Västergötland.

229 BARS, bronze, containing more copper than usual. – Unknown provenance.

230 GOLD HOARD, 47 gold coins (solidi) and a bracelet correspon-
ding to 17 solidi. – Helgö, Ekerö, Uppland.

231 BRONZE BARS. – Myrvälde, Tingstäde, Gotland.

232 PAIR OF SCISSORS, iron, for cutting of metal sheets. – Vallstena,
Gotland.

233 PAIR OF SCISSORS, like No. 232 above. – Skansen, Kalmar, Småland.

234 PAIR OF TONGS, iron. – Svarta Jorden, Birka, Uppland.

235 IMPLEMENT for making iron nails. – Martebo Myr, Lummelunda,
Gotland.

236 HAMMER, iron. – Hägvalds, Vallstena, Gotland.

237 SMALL HAMMERS for working with precious metals, iron. –
Svarta Jorden, Birka, Uppland.

238 WHETSTONES, sandstone, slate. – Svarta Jorden, Birka, Uppland.

239 MOLD, soapstone, for casting of metal bars.
MOLD, sandstone.
Svarta Jorden, Birka, Uppland.

240 CRUCIBLES, fired clay. – Helgö, Ekerö, Uppland.

241 CRUCIBLES, fired clay. – Svarta Jorden, Birka, Uppland.

242 HEAT SHIELD for a bellows, fired clay. – Svarta Jorden, Birka,
Uppland.

243 WHEEL for a drill, stone. – Svarta Jorden, Birka, Uppland.

244 WHEELS for polishing and cleaning. – Svarta Jorden, Birka,
Uppland.

245 ANVILS, iron, for a smith. – Mästermyr, Silte, Gotland.

246 STAMP SUPPORT, iron, like No. 245 above.

247 STAMP, iron, for impressing hour glass formed adornments like
No. 245 above.
STAMP SUPPORT, lead, belonging to No. 247 above.

248 STAMP SUPPORT?, iron, like No. 245 above.

249 STAMP, iron, like No. 245 above.

250 GRAVING TOOL, iron, like No. 245 above.

251 IMPLEMENT for making iron nails, iron, like No. 245 above.

252 PAIR OF TONGS, iron, like No. 245 above.

253 IMPLEMENT for stamping metal sheets, iron, like No. 245 above.

254 FILES, iron, like No. 245 above.

255 IMPLEMENT for cleaning soldered joints, like No. 245 above.

256 BROOCH, silver, stamped, gilded silver plates in repoussé. 250–
350 A.D. – Ryet, Strangsered, Västergötland.

257 PENDANT, gold, filigrée and granulation. 2nd century A.D. –
Överbo, Varnhem, Västergötland.

258 FINGER RING, gold, inset stone (cornelian) and stamped decorations. 4th century A.D. – Fullerö, Gamla Uppsala, Uppland.

259 DRINKING HORN MOUNTINGS, bronze, cast, with stamped decorations. 2nd century A.D. – Ardaghs, Ekeby, Gotland. (Modern
reconstruction)

56

260 CLASP BUTTONS, bronze, cast in two different molds, gilded. 450–550 A.D. – Havor, Hablingbo, Gotland.

261 BROOCH, silver, gilded, cast and then engraved, edgings nielloed. 5th century A.D. Häste, Rödön, Jämtland.

262 BROOCH, silver, gilded, cast. 5th century A.D. – Röra, Bohus-län.

263 BROOCH, silver, gilded, cast. 5th century A.D. – Provenance unknown, Skåne.

264 DRINKING HORN MOUNTINGS, bronze, stamped and gilded bronze sheets in repoussé, edgings plated with silver. 6th century A.D. – Söderby Karl, Uppland. (Modern reconstruction)

265 MOUNTINGS, bronze, gilded cast and then stamped and engraved. 7th century A.D. – Vallstena, Gotland.

266 EQUIPMENT from a woman's grave, Gotland. 8th century A.D.

267 EQUIPMENT from a man's grave, Uppland. 7th–8th century A.D

268 GOLD SMITH'S HAMMER. – Helgö, Ekerö, Uppland.

269 SPEAR HEAD, iron, inlaid with silver and copper. 10th century A.D. – Birka, Uppland.

270 STIRRUP, iron, inlaid with copper and brass. 10th century A.D. – Birka, Uppland.

271 DRESS PIN, silver, gilded, cast, partly inlaid with niello. 10th century A.D. – Birka, Uppland.

272 PENANNULAR BROOCH, bronze, cast, partly gilded and partly plated with white metal. 10th century A.D. – Birka, Uppland.

273 TORTOISE BROOCH, bronze, cast, gilded and partly plated with silver, details inlaid with niello. 9th century A.D. – Birka, Uppland.

274 TORTOISE BROOCH, bronze, cast, gilded, silver-plated and nielloed details, adorned with twisted silver threads. 9th century A.D. – Birka, Uppland.

275 TORTOISE BROOCH, bronze, cast, gilded silver-plated and nielloed details adorned with twisted silver threads. 9th century A.D. – Birka, Uppland.

276 EQUALARMED BROOCH, bronze, cast, gilded and adorned with twisted silver thread. 850–950 A.D. – Birka, Uppland.

277 EQUALARMED BROOCH, bronze, cast, silver-plated edgings. 850–950 A.D. – Birka, Uppland.

278 CRUCIFIX PENDANT, silver with filigrée and granulation. 10th century A.D. – Birka, Uppland.

279 NECKLACE, cornelian, rock crystal, glass silver pendants. 850–950 A.D. – Birka, Uppland.

280 EAR SPOON, silver, cast, partly gilded. 10th century A.D. – Birka, Uppland.

281 EQUESTRIAN FIGURES, silver. 10th century A.D. – Birka, Uppland.

282 SPUR, iron and bronze, inlaid with twisted silver and copper threads, 2nd century A.D. – Gärdslösa, Öland.

57

283 SPUR, bronze, inlaid with silver. 2nd century A.D. – Gärdslösa, Öland.

284 PENDANT, gold, with filigrée and granulation. 2nd century A.D. – Unknown provenance, Öland.

286 BROOCH, gilded silver, cast and then engraved, nielloed details. 450–550 A.D. – Unknown provenance, Gotland.

287 THORS HAMMER, silver, with filigrée and granulation. 11th century A.D. – Unknown provenance, Skåne.

Cover illustration:
Brooch, gilded silver, 6th century.
Svennevad, Närke.

© Copyright Historiska Museet Stockholm 1964
Kungl. Boktryckeriet P. A. Norstedt & Söner
Stockholm 1965